As you are reading these messages,

just remember,

always remember,

every single word, the whole book,

points directly to...

you

and what you are...

NOT.

Because of putting emphasis on some particular point, always we have trouble. We should accept things just as it is.

Suzuki Roshi

You are perfect just the way you are... and you could use a little improvement.

Suzuki Roshi

Poetry. We think of the poetry forced on us in school. A few short lines, usually in groups of four, and always rhyming. Just the word alone makes me cringe...or at least it used to. But what is poetry really?

Poetry can be much more. A single poem can say it all. A poem can be succinct precision on the end of a pin. Well performed, it is magic. And poetry isn't just words. It's around us always. Flashes of lightening in a night-time sky is poetic. Waves crashing on a rocky shore. Snow wind-whipped across a mountain summit. A flock of geese heading south. Kids playing tag. These are but a few examples of life in forever ongoing poetic motion.

Coming across a very simple and precise way of writing poetry changed my view of it. "Haiko" is a Japanese style using only three lines of 5/7/5 syllables. So things need to be simple and precise. Fewer words actually says more because the wording used and the crispness of the structure is strict and allows for no excess blabbing on endlessly when less is the key to the message. Simplicity, the key to life itself.

Most of the poems offered here are of the Haiko style. Some are of the "Waka" style, another Japanese form using five lines of 5-7-5-7-7 syllables. Others yet are laid down as they came, through the pen, and onto paper.

All I know is that I didn't come up with them. They came *through* me.

"Poetry" is a word that tries to describe something special. I prefer the word "magic".

Enjoy these messages. Have a conversation with them. Play with them.

Oliver, BC
March 7, 2015

WALKING
THE
PATH

Connections

The wolf and the loon must be brothers.
Listen to their cry.

The tree and the soil must be brothers.
Look at their roots.

All the colours must be brothers.
Look at the rainbow.

The moon and the pond must be bothers.
Look at their reflection.

The bees and the flowers must be
brothers.
Look at their honey.

Singing and music must be brothers.
Listen to the melody.

The wind and the wheat must be
brothers.
Look at the gentle flow.

The earth and the moon must be
brothers.
Look at the ocean tides.

Kids and puppies must be brothers.
Look at their happiness.

The trees and the winds must be
brothers.
Look at their dance.

Fire and wood must be brothers.
Look at their swirling smoke.

Canvas and paint must be brothers.
Look at the artistic work.

The rivers and the earth must be
brothers.
Look at the beautiful valleys.

The rain and the soil must be brothers.
Look at the plants grow.

Streams and rocks must be brothers.
Listen to the soft gurgling.

The wind and the ocean must be
brothers.
Look at the waves form.

Rain showers and the sky must be
brothers.
Look at the colourful rainbow.

What If

What if I could be the colour purple?
Then I'd be able to see how the other
colours feel.

What if I could be an eagle?
Then I'd be able to see what the other birds
see.

What if I was the wind?
Then I'd be able to see how a breeze feels
on a face.

What if I was a mirror?
Then I'd be able to see what reflects in me.

What if I could be silence?
Then I'd be able to hear for the first time.

What if I could be the moon?
Then I'd be able to see my reflection in a
pond.

What if I could be a cloud?
Then I'd be able to see both the sky and the
earth.

What if I could be a pair of shoes?
Then I'd be able to feel the earth beneath.

What if I could be a bee?
Then I could make love to all the beautiful
flowers.

What if I could be the great Pyramids?
Then I could have seen thousands of years
of history.

What if I could be you?
Then I would envy me.

What if I could be a smile?
Then I would feel the warmth of romantic
light.

What if I could be peace?
Then I would see how senseless war is.

What if I could be a fine wine?
Then I'd age to perfection.

What if I was music?
Then I'd see how music feels.

What if I was a rainbow?
Then I'd find the pot of gold.

What if I was laughter?
Then I could make everyone smile.

What if I was?
Then I would be.

<u>Be Still, Be Silent</u>

Be still.
Quiet.
Just breath.
Be silent.
Feel.
Listen.
Sense.

Ssshh.

Let it all be.
Experience.
Awaken.
Stop the noise.
Stop the chatter.
Quiet the mind.

Ssshh.

Let it come.
Let it be.
Be silent.
No talking.
No giving.
Just being.
Relax.
Enjoy it.
Be in the garden of life.
Breath deeply.
Breath slowly.
Be still.
Be silent.

Ssshhh.

The Buddha

A great man

Of infinite wisdom

Saw.

Labelling

Cloud does not know "cloud";
Mountain does not know "mountain".
We attach with words.

A Stream To One

A stream to one
With its bubbling waters
Is a river to another
And that's all that matters.

Something difficult to one
With all its toughness
Is a small matter to another
For it was seen in simpleness.

A fence to one
Helping to keep things in
Is a wall to another
For the sake of keeping out sin.

A hill to one
With its softness and curve
Is a mountain to another
Which takes away his nerve.

A book of religion to one
Giving him meaning to life
Is blasphemy to another
To be torn apart with a knife.

A simple plot of land to one
Used by his family to feed
Is a battleground to another
A place to test his mighty steed.

A freedom fighter to one
With a heart so righteous and brave
Is a terrorist to another
Who murders and forces peace to crave.

It is time to see that another's view
Is a similar side of one's belief
Where the two are much the same
Creating in all a sense of relief.

One includes another
Another includes the one
All views must be shared
For us all to live under the sun.

Small Mind

coarse and fine
big and small
tall and short
thin and thick
hot and cold
black and white
light and dark
good and bad
smart and dumb
time and timeless.

All false,
without existence.

Man made,
for his simple mind.

Taken Away

We are like a wave on a dark sea,
Tiny and light.
Once there, then gone,
Merged with the greater depths.

Our lives are blown about by our mind
Much like a wispy plume of snow
Taken to nowhere far away
From the mountain summit.

What Happened To Us?

Some time ago when things were slow
A generation had things to say, things to
show.
We wanted to bring about change
Without having everything feel so
strange.

We didn't want to make the most of it
We wanted to change things just a bit.
We had the ideas, had the notions
We wanted to do more than just go
through the motions.

Protesting against what we didn't like
At times went higher than a kite.
With ideals odd to some
We knew positive things would come.

So we took to the steps
And there would make our bets
That we could improve the world
And teach it not to use the sword.

We fought against foreign conflict,
Used a bigger environmental stick,
Voted to change those with powers
And lived a lifestyle against strangers in
the towers.

Our vision was clear
For we knew how to steer.
We would call on this planet
To change it into a sonnet.

Others' greed and apathy
Did not receive our sympathy.
For we would be different and would fight
Toward the proper goal and what was
right.

We used our music to get out the point
But at times we lost track because of the
joint.
The message was clear by the strength
of our voices
But at times we were confused with too
many choices.

But as the Leavers began to age
We became Takers and began to change.
We gave up our belief
And many began looking like a thief.

All too soon we became
Just like the others, all the same.
We had become what we had hated
When power and money had us baited.

What happened to us
Is that we got on the same bus
To a place of greed and power
Giving up our soul and our flower.

We went on to consume
With an ego to presume
That we were better than those before
Because we used wealth as our score.

We shunned our beliefs of equality
We threw away our wish for simplicity.
We no longer found things so strange
For we had insured there was to be no
change.

Just Doing

When the wind blows through the trees...listen

When the moon reflects on the still pond below...see

When the rose sends out its fragrance...smell

When the sheep gives away its wool...feel

When drinking a precious tea...taste

When walking on slippery ice...balance

When resting on a wooden chair...sit

When by the edge of a cliff...stand

When moving through the forest...walk

No thinking...just doing

Not two...Not one

A Planet Dies

A planet dies, giving, giving
So man lives, taking, taking
A simple ball with limited space
With an end in sight to what it has.

A planet dies, hurting, hurting
So man lives, singing, singing
With an ego of endless wants
With no end in sight to what it picks.

Rivers black, mountainsides bare
Lands scorched, not even clean is the air
When will man see he is the one
To cause all the problems, to block out
the sun.

When will we see we are too many
For soon we will have none, not any
We are Takers and not Leavers
We must change and become Retrievers.

What will we drink when waters are only
tide
And what will we eat when soil cannot
provide
Where will we live when we cannot find
shelter
And what will we breathe when air is
helter-skelter?

What of all the animals already here
How do we alleviate all their fear
What do we do to save the plants
And all the beings and little ants?

<u>Consider This</u>

Consider this.
      Our world destroyed by greed
      Wars fought for reasons forgotten
      Children receiving no schooling
      Poor people dying deceased
      Clean water becoming scarce
      Problems with too many people.

I've said too much already.
      But listen to the earth cry
      Listen to the homeless refugees
      Listen to an ignorant child
      Listen to the dying wail
      Listen to the trickle of a once mighty
river
      Listen to the constant noise of voices.

I've thought too much already.
      But think of species gone
      Think of the result of hatred
      Think of grinding hopelessness
      Think of wasted lives
      Think of parched lands
      Think of the skeletons of the hungry.

I've seen too much already.
      But see the forests shrink
      See the destruction of homes
      See the poverty continue

See the orphans of the dead
See the deserts advancing
See the destruction caused by so
many.

I've heard too much already.
But hear the planet choking
Hear the cries of the maimed
Hear the silence of children
Hear the stillness of death
Hear the anger of the thirsty
Hear the screaming over fewer
resources.

I've felt too much already.
But feel the filth around us.
Feel the fear and hatred of history
Feel the toughness of life
Feel the loneliness of lost families
Feel the crusty arid soil
Feel the tension in the air.

Consider that
Only we can stop polluting.
Only we can stop hating.
Only we can stop ignorance.
Only we can stop disease.
Only we can stop abuse.
Only we can stop ourselves.

Song of the Ego

I WANT it ALL!

I WANT it ALL!
And I want it NOW!
I want all things I see to feed my need to
have more than you!

I want to win it ALL!
And I want to win it NOW!
I want to win at everything to feed my
need to be better than you!

I want to always feel GOOD!
And I want to feel good NOW!
I want to be admired to feed my need to
feel that I can be better than you!

I want more POWER!
And I want it NOW!
I want to be all-powerful to feed my need
to be stronger than you!

I want ATTENTION!
And I want it NOW!
I want to have more attention to feed my
need to feel more liked than you!

I want it ALL!
And I want it NOW!
I don't care what I have as long as it's
more than you to feed my need to feel
bigger!

Once I have it ALL
And once I have it NOW
I'll be able to brag to feed my need to be
heard.

Once I have it ALL
And once I have it NOW
I'll demand more to feed my never
ending appetite for...

The City

The rush to race starts early
With artificial light to show the way
Pushing for space stolen from another
At speeds that kill with sudden stops.

The rush to race continues
In the tall cement cages
Where deceit is the special of the day
Until one is gone followed by laughter
from another.

The rush to race follows late
With artificial lighting light showing the
way
Pushing for space stolen from another
At speeds that kill with sudden stops.

The rush to race is taken outside
Toward the quiet places
Where the pushing goes on for space
In a small town where locals turn away.

All too soon, the race begins again
Back to the place they love to hate
Where the pushing goes on for space
Where they dread the rush to race.

The Lost Inheritance

The world, left alone, is a wonder
but we, with our greed, put it asunder.

First came the wars and all the fighting
with all the destruction taking away the lighting.

Then came land, water and air overuse;
all we had learned was violent abuse.

The land and the animals have not done this;
we alone are at fault for nearing the abyss.

There is still time to bring earth back to a range
but only we can do it, only we can change.

Wanting To Do It All

The slowness of getting here is slowed.
The rush of staying here is rushed.
The wall of blackness is getting closer
Creating a need to do it and to do it now.

Living between when things were done
And the time of no longer doing
Is a time of confusion of what should be
stopped,
Of what should be started.

Thoughts of what was
Reliving memories of old
While thinking of what is to be
And dreaming of a foggy new path.

I am in wonderland
Wanting to do it all
Wanting to do it now
But slowed by the heaviness of time.

I go up much more slowly
I come down much more satisfied.
My senses have been refocused
Shaping new memories of old to relive.

Perfection is not the reason
It is finally simply the doing.
A single step or a mountain summit are
the same
Sipping tea and clawing ice are no
different.

Without a list of doing to keep
The mind settles into the Mind
Where my all is part of the All
When happiness journeys to Joy.

Less Than Us

Walking into the space we call our own
The man drops his life onto the floor.
The soft thump of his belongings raises
the dust
From the unkempt floor where his life
now lays.

We stare at the man of dubious means
With a sideways glance that misses his
view.
The stranger is nervous and makes us
squirm
So we try not to hear when he
approaches to speak.

Our bodies are tense because he is close
So we plan our escape should he make a
move.
He speaks in riddles which confirms our
fears
That this man is different and less than
us.

With a nervous giggle and a curt reply
We hope to look invisible to this
stranger.
He moves away to our sighs of relief
Not sure what to do with his silence of
rejection.

We watch him hover with his sense of
loss
Relieved to see him leave with his life in
a bag.
We're quick to talk about the strange
man
Walking out of the space we call our
own.

<u>Fake</u>

My life is not here to soothe your soul.
Like the pond under the moon
My feelings toward you
Only reflect what you really are
Not the lie on how you want to be seen.

Your intentions are false.
Your lies are real.
Your pretensions are of a fool.
Your exaggerations are from fear.

Others will decide what you really are
Long before you stop your endless
words.

The View of a Distant Friend

You understand nothing of me.
What do you think you see?
The vision you want?
The vision you need?
What is it you want to see?
You want me to be what you thought me
to be
but disappointed by your failure to see
me for what I need to be.
Not pulled by you, not pulled by me
there is a view only I can see
which is to say I could be a tree.

The world changes, furious and fast
only to be concerned of the future and
past.
There is another way, calm and slow
which leads up the Way. Go!

As sure as the target draws the arrow,
so does the Way attract the marrow
of the one willing to see
that we can be anything, including a
tree.

<u>There</u>

I am going, to be "there".

But "there" is where?

A place beyond, a place to be?

No.

You see, there is no other

Since "there" is actually...

here.

<u>Look Inside Your Heart</u>

We are what is in our heart
And actions follow emotions.
We are what we think
And actions follow thoughts
We are what we say
And actions follow speech.
We are what we do
And reactions follow actions.

Let an emotion arise
Let a thought surface
Let speech come out
...and action soon follows.

Look inside your heart.

My Father's Eyes

When I look into my father's eyes
Little by little I now realize
What he has seen, what he has lived.

When I look into my father's eyes
I see his soul, conquered by life
His desperation in hard times
His fears in battles of war
His efforts in raising a family
His sadness from leaving home.

When I look into my father's eyes
He shows me why he is tired
He tells me he wishes soon to go.

Winds of Emotion

Lost in the winds of emotion...
We are all lost in the winds of emotion.

Angered by others' foolishness,
Pushed by the greed of the few.
Led by those in power,
Like a ship of fools without oars.
Learning to hate for fear of others,
We fight for reasons unknown.
Flying to space to escape here,
While leaving behind many to starve.
Raping our home for the things we want,
We will leave nothing for what we need.
Our souls are empty vessels,
With no grasp of the only One.

Lost in the winds of emotion...
We are all lost in the winds of emotion.

Colours of Mist

The mist covers all
In shades of white, grey and black.
Colours are...
asleep.

Is It?

Is it simple?
Is it very complicated?
It is really neither.

__Not On A Map__

The way to the place
Which is simple and normal
Is not on a map.

Nothing More

The river washes the soil.
The wind brushes the grass.
The season colours the surface.
The rain cleans the air.
The sun warms us all.
Nothing more!

<u>Stop and Become</u>

Running, rushing, going fast
All to no avail
Catching nothing but wrinkles.
Nothing to grasp,
Nothing to keep
Except wanting and needing.
Where satisfaction never comes
And happiness is a myth.

Stop!

If cloud's catch your sun's warmth,
Become the clouds.
If the fox hunts your food,
Become the fox.

This moment is simple!

The Mountains Don't Care

The city bubbles.
Noise and people and traffic.

The mountains don't care.

Be Flexible

Strong wind moves green leaves
While the yurt stands firm and round.
Be flexible and deflect.

Same Roots

The elm soars in pride
The willow hangs down
                    ...in shame
Both from the same source.

<u>Labelling</u>

Cloud does not know "cloud"
Mountain does not know "mountain".
We attach with words.

Forest Fog

The forest wears a cloak
Fog softly surrounds all life.
Wet yellow leaves cry.

All Things Are One

The sound of one hand
Is Buddha nature.

Do you know what it is?
You must find it
Though you haven't lost it.

There it is! Can you see it?
Here it is! Can you smell it?
There it is! Can you hear it?
Here it is! Can you taste it?
There it is! Can you feel it?
Here it is! Can you touch it?
There it is! Can you sense it?

It is everything!
It is everywhere!
It is always!

All things are together as One.
Your Original Face,
Before thoughts, before thinking!

The interconnected web of existence with
its impermanence
Is the sound of one hand,
Is Buddha nature.
And you are part of it influencing and
being influenced.

Say it less.
Experience it more.
Right here!
Right now!

A Reflection

A man walks toward me
As a reflection in a window.
Is it less real than the man?
Both are reflections of my mind.
Both are reality of Mind.
Distorted reflection by the window,
Distorted reflection by the mind.

Problem Thoughts

Don't have any problems
All I have are problem thoughts.
No thoughts, no problems.

Refection of a Light

From the darkness
A lamp pushes back the night
And shines on the river below.
From the other side
I see a reflected line.
I move, the reflection moves;
Far this way, far that way
So all the river reflects the light.
Reality is like that.
We see the one way
When there is the One way.

Roishi's Deer

We eat in silence.
A deer enters Roshi's mind.
Does he know it's there?

<u>See When Not Looking</u>

One thought...too many!
Can only See when not looking.
See...don't look; don't point.

Age By Ego Again

The neighbour walks in
Tight clothes to be ageless.
Fooled by the ego.

Shrinking mind, Expanding Mind

Everything is slowing
Knowing nothing happens outside the
mind.
The mind is shrinking
Shining brilliantly
Heading toward the center of brightness
The center of mind
Now smaller than its container.
Everything outside it is softening
Knowing nothing happens outside the
Mind.
The Mind is expanding
Taking All in
And becoming a single thing
The One encompassing All.

Wind and Snow

Wind plays with the snow,
Slim tall trees bend back and forth.
Where does it come from?
Where does it decide to go?
It just comes and goes like wind.

<u>Sonoma Zendo</u>

The Zendo is life
And it is where I belong
Listening to nothing, hearing all
Looking for nothing, seeing all.
The Zendo is the mother of zazen
Zazen is the mother of me.
The Zendo breathes life
And I inhale it deeply.

Wind Buffets Seagull

The seagull is buffeted by the wind.
It saves energy by holding firm,
No flapping of the wings.
Angry winds go around it
Like turbulent waters around boulders.
I can learn from this.

<u>Zendo Noise</u>

Zazen in the zendo
Scratching noise on the roof
Is it a large squirrel
Or is it my small mind?

All Is In Mind

It came to me while sitting still
There is no thing outside my mind
I am apart from everything
I am a part of everything
Changes come and changes go
I am what I see
I see what I am

A Thought

The ocean's tide rises,
A wave rushes over the sand bar,
Turns into fuzzy foam
And disappears into the sand.
As a thought,
It has come and gone.

Change the World

I can change the world
Anytime I decide to change
The thoughts that are mind.

Feeding Thoughts

The senses feed the mind
To satisfy the hunger of thoughts
Poisoning the mind.

There Is Only Nowhere

There is nowhere to hide;
Certainly not inside this skinbag.

There is nowhere to get lost;
Certainly not outside this skinbag.

There is nowhere to go;
There is nowhere to be.

There is only no-where.
There is only no-where...here.

<u>Stranger In A Strange Land</u>

The truth has been found,
the truth to set me free.
The raft from the other shore
has been sent back
to help others also be free.

Now seeing the other shore is sad.
Sad to see how others are,
how they need to change
simply.
Living in their land
surrounded by their ways
is hard.

I am a stranger in a strange land
screaming inside
again.
But this time to show
what the truth really is
inside.

If you travel blindly
you will fall
often.
If you push others
storms will come your way
coldly.

The world is living in a dream
but now we know we can
change.
There is a life of simplicity
by knowing the mind called
the way.

Take the ride with me
to the other shore
to savour
freedom.
Become a stranger in a strange land
lead others by example
safely.
Shed light on the dark night
for all.

A Clear View

A fortress,
    made of walls.
One less thought,
    one less brick.
Soon,
    a clear view.

Mysterious Encounter

Had a mysterious encounter
    today
Similar ones being felt
    everyday.
Can't see it.
Can't touch it.
Can't hear it.
Can't smell it.
Can't taste it.
Can't understand it.
But...huh...
    there it is again.
A thought.

The Dream Is The Answer

I thought I saw it
I thought I thought I saw it
Was it just a dream?
I thought I felt it
I thought I thought I felt it
Was it just a dream?
Then there was the feeling
The feeling I knew the answer
Was it just a dream?
Then I finally realized
The dream is the answer
Knowing it's a dream is the answer.
I'm satisfied I've said too much.

The Source of All

It's never too late
    to feel the source
    that is all there is.
It is always with you
    so close at hand
    with you here and now.
The source of all things
    whose eyes you must open
    is your very own mind.

Watch

Watch the seagull glide happily.
Watch the stream bubble happily toward home.
Watch the cloud kiss the mountain.
Just Watch.
Smell the red rose.
Smell the earth.
Smell the field of wheat.
Just Smell.
Feel the warmth of the flame.
Feel the breeze caressing your skin.
Feel for others.
Just Feel.
Taste slowly the tea.
Taste vividly the water.
Taste the air.
Just Taste.
Listen to your breath.
Listen to the tree grow.
Listen to the mind lock open.
Just Listen.

Mind...

Mind...
Tell me...
What are you looking for?

Reflect What Is

Your mind reads with all your senses
Which do not judge.
Only when judgements take place,
Only when preferences are given
Do attachments happen.
Stop clinging!
Stop judging!
Be the transparent mirror.

<u>**Start Here**</u>

It is difficult
To save all sentient beings.
Maybe I'll start here.

The Eyes of Truth

The truth, simple and full,
Cannot be understood
Cannot be grasped
Until there is a return to innocence
Through the eyes of truth
Seeing the original mind
Believing in nothing
Knowing all.

Become Awareness

The incessant chatter
The incessant rushing
All to busy the mind.
Stop!
Stop this madness!
Return to the emptiness
Become awareness.

<u>Bus To Where</u>

Leaning on his cane
A man looks out the window
On a bus to where?

Cat Zen

A black cat is focused on its prey.
Another black cat, staring piercingly,
Readying its instincts to pounce when ready.
And then it happens;
Front paws holding firm
Back paws punishing the other
Until the moment to end it all comes
By licking the other in affection.
The kill and the love
Are both and equally
Cat Zen.

Pink Blackness

Where does the pink of a sunset come from?
It wasn't here all day.
The night that follows readies the next day
To invite back the pink
Before it turns to blackness
Once again.

Seagull Sunset

The sunset results
In a softness beyond words
While the seagull shits.

<u>Seeing More Clearly</u>

The tree-ness of a tree,
The mountain-ness of a mountain,
Make them what they are.
The snow covering both is white
Because it is no other colour.
All is calm here
As clouds flow by.
My tired eyes now see more clearly,
Even during the coming of night.

Shedding the Skin Bag

A stinky skin bag
Washes its mind with dharma
Shedding its old form,
Dropped away
Like a useless leaf in the autumn.

Teaching Nothing

My teacher teaches me
     by doing
     nothing.
Yet I learn by watching.
Yet I learn by listening.
My teacher teaches me
     by saying
     nothing.
He is.
I am.

The Result

Memories from the past,
From my ancestors,
Form the weather system
That is me.
With the sun above,
The world turning under my feet,
The darkness waits to greet the stars.
I am the result
Of all that comes
Before the equals sign.

All In Turn

Thirsty trees lick rain.
Fog embraces the mountain.
Blue skies wait their turn.

All Oceans Are One

We name oceans
To differentiate them.
But they know
Their waters are interconnected
And thus
Are one.

Mind Source

Arriving home
Mind empty of fullness
Now full of emptiness
The mind is all,
The source of all things.

Mind of Mirrors

The untrained mind
Is a damp cave of angled mirrors
Reflecting all things differently.
Confusion!
A trained mind
Has no mirrors or walls
Being open to anything.
Clarity!

The Mind's Root

All roots are strong
From the root of the tallest tree
To the root of the shortest grass.
Find the root of your mind.
Where does it grow from?

The Rudder of Zen

Leaving the shore of knowns,
Or so it seems,
In a one person boat
Heading toward the other shore,
Or so it seems.

Soon the winds of thought
Stirs the mind's waters
Sending the boat
To unknown places,
In unknown directions,
Or so it seems.

There is no way to manage,
Or so it seems,
Until the rudder of Zen
Directs this message in a bottle
To the shore of truths,
The same shore
Where the boat was built.

Endless Essence

As fish swimming in an endless sea
Like birds flying in an endless sky
So we live in an endless essence.

Guiding the Ox

My ox has escaped again.
As quickly as knowing it
I stand beside it as a friend,
Hand on its shoulder
Guiding it back
To its resting place.

It escapes less often now.
Its body becoming lighter and softer
Easier to guide home
Where it now stays longer
Resting with eyes ready
Looking for a way out.

It will always find escapes
To the outside it knows so well
Though now more than ever
It stays in its home
Translucent and light
Happy just to observe.

<u>Only Now</u>

Living in fear
Is living in the past.
Fear can only come from the past.

Living in hope
Is living in the future.
Hope can only come from the future.

Living in reality
Is living in the present.
Realty can only come from the present.

Dry Stone In Wet Water

A stone in a river
Is always dry.
It is only the water
That is wet.

Our essence
Is always still.
It is the mind
That is thinking.

It is the thought
That bubbles up.
Created from nothing,
Going nowhere.

Mind, like water,
Always wet.
Essence, like the stone,
Always dry.

<u>Words Don't Reach</u>

Words cannot reach this world,
The world beyond the Absolute.
Nothing more to say.

Bell Speak

The Zen student strikes.
The bell sounds and the hills answer.
The mind has spoken.

The Word Trap

If the human mind conceives it
It cannot be so.
Beware of the word given it.
It will entrap you
As a spider's web ensnares a wild tiger
While it keeps a safe distance.

Be Stuck

The student says he is stuck.
Then be "stuck" he is told
And feel the "stuck".
The plateau the student is on
Frustrates him
Only making "stuck" stronger.
Not seeing the "stuck"
As the penetration of the previous lesson
Only comes from the small mind.
Big Mind does not care.
Let the "stuck" teach as well as any
lesson.
Welcome it home.

The Dance of Nature

The leaves shake themselves
Dancing with the passing wind.
The universe sings.

The Weary Willow

A heavy fog encloses the willow tree
Dragging down its wispy limbs
In heavy sadness.
Without help it can only wait.

A soft breeze appears
Gently moving the tips of limbs
Slowly returning to life.

The strengthening breeze
Heightens the dance of happiness
Until the willow waves goodbye
To its lover moving on back to blue sky.

<u>Do Not Judge</u>

Feel the wind
    from a soft breeze
    to a strong cyclone
    and do not judge
    good or bad.

Taste the flavour
    from a sweet tea
    to a hot pepper
    and do not judge
    good or bad.

Hear the sound
    from a low hum
    to a loud scream
    and do not judge
    good or bad.

Smell the odour
    from a mature rose
    to fresh dung
    and do not judge
    good or bad.

See the sights
        from a bright sunset
        to a dull grey sky
        and do not judge
        good or bad.

Experience the sensations
        with all they offer
        and do not judge
        good or bad.

As ice and steam
        are both water
        do not judge
        good from bad.

Time Comes, Time Goes, Time Returns

Time runs out from where we are.
Time runs out from the present
To the past
To the future.
Time runs out from the past
To the present.
Time runs out from the future
To the present.
Time goes where it wants
As myriad streams dance through the
delta of life
On their way home.
Time always comes back to us.
We and time are one.

Wiping Nothing

The dust of greed irritates the eyes
Producing the crying of graying sadness
When things are not gained.
We think we are blinded
By the mirror-covering dust of endless
delusions.
Going ever forward,
Wanting to attain freedom
By trying to wipe the mirror clean.
We finally see
There is nothing to attain,
Because there is no dust, no mirror.
So shatter the mirror that isn't,
Throw away the dust that is not,
In the place of the Unborn.

<u>Sun and Moon Dance</u>

The sun comes around
With its warmth and with its light;
Its time is short-lived.
The moon pushes aside the sun
To bounce from the waters below.

Poor Weakling

Bones
Stacked oddly
Bleached
Held together by a skin bag.
But with a single thought
Become large and strong
Full of greed, anger and ignorance
Able to destroy
......itself.

Takers

You drink my wine and eat my crops
Ply my seas and fly my skies
Move me with harshness
To take what you want.

   My air suffers
   My water thickens
   My land cries out
   My animals disappear
   My plants wither

Never done kindly
Never done softly
You are all Takers
Few are ever Leavers.

   My air suffers
   My water thickens
   My land cries out
   My animals disappear
   My plants wither

As you wish and without care
You waste my rivers
Fill my gorges
Cloud my skies.

     My air suffers
     My water thickens
     My land cries out
     My animals disappear
     My plants wither

All to please
     the greed
     in you.

Everyone Said

She said he said
He said she said...
All is false
All is confused.
The way to honesty is not this
Honesty is not that.

They said she said
He said they said.
Repeating it differently
Brings out falseness.
Anger and ignorance
Raise their ugly heads.

We said he said
They said she said
He said they said
She said we said.

How can truth be told
When,
She said he said
He said they said
They said we said
We said she said.

A Playful Wind

The wind blows through my mind
Surfing the hills and valleys
Dancing with the palm tree.
The waterfall rides the gusts
Splashing my face.
There is glee in all this.
The palm tree, the waterfall and I
Thank the playful wind.

Unknowable

Words do not express.
Seeing is too late.
Hearing cannot grasp.

Those who say they speak, see or hear
Are mistaken.
They throw themselves into the torrent
Without knowing how to swim.

The Great Truth includes all
Even the world's dust.
There is always complete truth
Whether dust is or isn't.

What is it?
The relative or the absolute?
Neither.
Both.
Neither.

The old skin-bag of India,
Buddha,
Sits on this cushion.

Be That

Hot comes...hot.
Cold comes...cold.
You can only be what is.

<u>Calmness</u>

When the eye does not see
And the ear does not hear
Only then is there calm.

Dancing Shadow

A palm tree shadow
Dances with joy through the day.
At night it rests.

No Island

Seeing the shore nearby
Believing to be alone
Living on an island
Surrounded by oceans.

Wondering, questioning,
Looking up
Seeing other islands
Separated only by streams.

Buddha lifts my chin
To see streams dried by the sun of wisdom
With a vast land encompassing all.
Only one, only the same.

<u>Once Only</u>

Clear night skies tickle
The blanket of black softness
Never to be seen again
Never seen before

<u>Warnings</u>

Rib-caged clouds pass by
With warnings of things to come.
Trees stand still, waiting.

Maturing Fruit

You will never see the wind
Or your own face.

But they do exist
And are part of you.
And the relative
And the absolute.

The fruit matures on a healthy tree.

<u>Once Again</u>

Hitch a ride on a lightning bolt.
Slide down a rainbow.
Grab a sunbeam's warmth.
Hug the moon's reflection.
Kiss the sky's blue.
Dance with a windblown palm tree.
Build a fire with a snow flake.

Do things that are natural,
Natural to the Zen mind.
Open your eyes and listen.
Open your ears and see.

And be your Original self,
Once again.

Here It Is!!

Confusion arrives...
Which way to simplify?
Oh wait!...

　　Here it is!

No Need To See

Crows fly by with grace
Looking nowhere, seeing all.
Which way should I go?
Trees blast green, sky blasts blue.
This chair is comfortable.

No Thinking

False thinking comes...uninvited
As heavy as stone
With the power of a tsunami.
Fool's gold shines
Easily attracting...the weak.
Don't invite.
Drink your tea.
Then smash the cup.

Only Being

Where to go?
There is nothing to attain...
    here.
There is nothing to attain...
          there.
There is nowhere to go...
    not here
        not there.
Only be
Only being
Here
Now

All There Is

Hello to you.
Let me introduce myself.
I've been around for a long long time.
I am the wind blowing through your hair,
The planet a thousand light-years away.
I am the darkness of form,
The brightness of emptiness.
I am the colour of everything,
The form of things to come.
I am time gone by,
The things yet to be.
I am you from before birth to after death,
The cause and effect of all this.
I am the absolute and the relative,
The inter-relationship of all things.
Nice to meet you.
Hope you know my name.

ANGER FELT!!

I FEEL **ANGRY**!
I SENSE TIGHTNESS!
I <u>AM</u> ANGER!!
I AM ANGER <u>ITSELF</u>!!
TIGHT CHEST!
I AM ANGRY!
But at what? At whom? Why?

A Master Lost

A Zen master losses his Way
Damning, pointing
Angrily defaming
Not wanting to let go
Of his very own anger
Of his very own ego.
What a loss!
He has lost.
He is lost.
But he is proof
Of the Buddha's teachings.

Being A Palm Tree

The palm tree sways
       to   and   fro
      without concern.
Being a palm tree must be simple
      must be nice.

The Storm

The storm awaits.

Greyness
Then night-like darkness
Descends
As the angry black army
Swirls
To lash its fury as
Rain
Harsh and pounding rain
Blinding
Forcing metal chariots to
Stop
And fear what cannot be
Controlled.

Ah, the power of nature
Eliminates
The human's frail
Ego.

Alone With Someone

Sometimes I think
    I should be alone.
Then I remember that I already am.

Sometimes I think
    I should be with someone.
Then I remember that's not possible.

Sometimes I think
    I should be alone with someone.
Then I remember that's the way it is.

And Us ???

A bird flies through the sky
Knowing of no beginning or end to the sky.
A fish swims through the ocean
Knowing of no beginning or end to the ocean.
Not knowing of life and death
A simple life is led.

And us ???

<u>No Begending</u>

Cause and effect...
It cannot be!
To have a cause
    there must be a beginning.
To have an effect
    there must be an end.
There is neither.
And there is not neither.

Meanwhile

Sparrows look for food
    and bath in the stony dust of time.
Olive trees are brushed
    by the breeze of change.
Flies search my legs
    for remnants of my aging.
Shadow's hide
    from the sun's motion.
Meanwhile...
    I don't exist.

Slow Down

Slow down everybody!
You can't get it all in,
You can't get it all done.
Tear up your list to beat.

Slow down everybody!
You're moving too fast,
You're killing your home.
Don't listen to your mind.

Slow down everybody!
Nothing can be gained,
Nothing will be lost.
Throw away your watch.

Slow down everybody!
You have nothing to prove,
You have nothing to improve.
Don't be afraid.

Slow down everybody!
Watch a stone change,
And play with the wind.
Smile at the magic of it all.

We Are Me, We Are You

Hello…again
It's you and me…again.
Can it ever be said
You aren't me
I'm not you?
We are me
We are you
All as one.

Nothing else to say.

Gotta Ask

Gotta ask yourself the question
    Where are ya now?
    Are ya here or are ya somewhere
you don't recognize?

Gotta ask yourself the question
    Who are ya now?
    Are ya who you think you are or are
ya someone else?

Gotta ask yourself the question
    When are ya now?
    Are ya being you now or are ya
doing some other time?

Gotta ask yourself the question
    What are ya doing now?
    Are ya doing what you think you
are or are you not?

Gotta ask yourself the question
    What is the real question?
    Is there even an answer?

The Human Sickness

Lips move constantly
        ….nothing is said.
Eyes look constantly
        ….nothing is seen.
Ears listen constantly
        ….nothing is heard.

Doing, doing, doing.

The human sickness.

Doing is the chatter
        ….of loneliness
        ….of fear
        ….of not being one.

Easy Stuff

can you...
climb a frozen waterfall in summer
go to bed with the rain
blow a gasket
grab a handful of the sky
make flour from bread
paint yourself invisible
chase a flock of headless horses
grow your hair in
get a white tan
turn ashes into wood
light up the day
cut a grassless field
melt steam
fly underground
swim in the sky
freeze the sun
get a sunflower to follow the moon
investigate nothing
live forever

...why not??

Finding a Way

finding a way
yes
finding a way.
I'll find way
to…
yes…
to use a way
to…
what?
I forgot.
was it to put an elephant on a diet?
invent dry water?
find intelligence in humans?
no
those are easy.
but I'll find a way
to…
find a way…

somehow

Fluff

fluff...
that's all there is
nothing else
is to be taken
seriously.
but fluff
says it all.
life, death and all before, during and
after...

is all fluff.

Going With Change

Destination?
There is none.
Only pathways
Some rocky
Others smooth
Some clear
Others dark
Some wide
Others narrow.
And always,
Always,
There is no stopping
Nor reversing
Only a-heading.
No searching
No stopping
No resting.
Impermanence pushes
Impermanence pulls
Toward change
In change
With change.
The circle of life and death
Continues.

Gurus All

Ah, the world according to gurus
    sounds all the same.
So many gurus speaking
    different languages
    spewing all the same.
"Come closer and I will show you
    the way to eternal bliss.
Come closer and I will
    pick your bones clean
    ready for the buzzards of
suffering."
So, all you innocents
    keep your distance.
Live as nature does
    with a simplicity
    toward all things.
Close your mouth
    open your ears.
Know and understand
    of feeling the way
    according to only you.

Life Never Ends

life,
the jam session that never ends
with loud base
and sour notes

life,
the weather system that hangs about
with clear skies
and sudden thunder

life,
the traveller's road that goes on forever
with narrow lanes
and sudden turns

<u>Scratch Your Neck</u>

scratch your neck
and you'll see
you'll know
nothing else
at that moment
is anywhere
near
as important...
unless!
there is pressure on your ankle
which lets you forget
that...
you...
ever...
scratched your neck

Sun, Moon, Shadow

sun chases shadow
    as an older brother plays with
    a sibling.
which way?
shadow never knows
    only giggles and runs
playfulness continues
    in the heat of the day

moon pushes shadow
    as an older brother
    coerces a sibling
which way?
shadow never knows
    only frowns and crawls
sluggishness continuing
    in the depth of night

Too Much Talking

language
talk
always exaggerating
always extra
always too much
but the wind and the sun
know what to say
how to say it
and
when to stop

Always!

humans
listen...
learn...
from the wind and the sun

Always!

A Fool's Thoughts

What holds up your parachute?
The wind?
What holds up the wind?
Thoughts?
Ha! You Fool!
There are none!

A Wilting Flower

She moves more slowly
Wilting ever faster
With the winds of time
In the winds of change.
Forgetfulness expands
Lost eyes more confused
With a disappointing presence
Part of the breeze of aging.
Confused more often
Speaking in damaged thoughts
Bringing a fear to come
Of a heartless stone death.
Mistakes cause her to giggle
To cover the concern
Of a life losing control
Forgotten,
Under a closing cold dark night.

Dancing Rain

the rain dances
on my umbrella
            giggling
                    laughing
        bouncing
            playing
until...
        it wets my feet

No-Thing

Is there anybody out there?
Is there anybody in here?
Is there anything out there?
Is there anything in here?
Searching
Searching
Always searching
For somebody, for something
Not finding
Not finding
Never finding
Anybody, anything
Why?
Why!?
Damn it! Why!!?
Look
Look no further
There is only no-one.
There is only no-thing.

Moroccan Sand Dunes

Shifting and still
Sculpted by the wind
Heated by the sun
Cooled by the night
With a gracefulness all their own
Softness
Kindness
Countless grains of sand
Little planets
Are as one
Just as all of us are...

On an endless journey

<u>Question and Answer</u>

It's not the answer to the Question
Or
The question to the Answer
But
A fear of finding the Truth
Sleeping at night to miss the cold darkness
Awake by day to see our foggy dreams

We are the Question
We are the Answer
We are the Truth
We can wake up from this fog
From this dream
To be
      Fully
           Awake

           NOW!

Senseless Chatter

Is it an angry wind?
Furious bees looking for a fight?
An angry sea battering a rocky coast?
None of these.
Constant chatter
By ignorants looking for acceptance
For a superior position.
Endless
Constant
Useless
Mindless
Chatter.
The deluded trudge
Chairs in hand
On which to sit and hide their laziness.
Slumped faces
Having to endure another useless
uneventful event
Listening to a stone's
Hypocrisy.
They are and represent the greatest
illness of all
That of the ego
Lost...
Inflated...
Flat...
Loud...
Painful.

A Key to Me

Found a key once.
It just appeared
Though was never not here.
I was simply blind.
A key...
To what?
To where?
To a gate?
Oh no.
To a gem box?
Oh no.
The key...
Was to me.
But the key and me
Never have been
Never will be...
Apart.

Going Where

Where's it all going?
Since there is no where to go
Stop planning to go.
Everywhere can only be here,
Everything is only here.

Knowing the Ungraspable

The ungraspable
Must be known without knowledge.
Like air, it is there.
Ghosts in the mist are still there.
Does exist. Cannot be expressed.

Only Absolute

Standing where i am
Presence flows through me as life.
Without thinking mind
Relative cannot exist.
Only Complete Absolute Presence.

Only the Doing

All things simply are,
All parts acting as one thing.
Nothing stops to be –
There is only the doing.
Which way to the market place?

Truth Is Always There

The truth is shadow,
You can never run away.
A tree knows better.
Face your shadow as the truth
Just as the tree flows with wind.

Waves of Disturbance

The deepest oceans have waves and
disturbance.
But just below the surface,
All the way to its final depth
The surface disturbance is not, is calm.
The waves are not of the seas
But caused by the winds of life.
Let the waves of living
Exist only on your surface
While not disturbing the deeper you.
There will always be winds of life
But as the forced winds of the afternoon heat
So too will the life's winds become calm.

Motion-less-ness

When you look at the peak
You forget the little things

When you look at the little things
You forget the peak

Let your youth push you forward
Let you elderness hold your hand

Know what you didn't at a young age
Let age smile at what you now know

Forget your achievements of time past
Forget not remembering them

Just watch the swaying of the wild grasses
As the winds of time flow around you

Look for the wind with no movement
Find the tree without roots

Clouds ask questions of the mountains
Trees whisper answers to the sky

The absolute speaks softly
The relative listens intently

Forget knowing everything
Know there is nothing to know

Blind and Dumb

Speed, speed, high on speed
Always running
Full of greed.

Walking in a shroud
Just not thinking
All are a foolish crowd.

Not a smile on any a face
Sadness built in
Crazy, crazy pace.

Going that way not to think
On autopilot
On the brink.

Cold outside, cold inside
Unaware of what there is
Wishing for a free ride.

On their soles or in metal tubes
Must go faster
What fools, what boobs.

Want to shake them to wake up
Let's go! Let's try!
May as well talk to a coffee cup.

Speed, speed, high on speed
Always running
Full of greed.

Here Is That Way

When it rains the riverbed stays dry
The mountains support the clouds
Grasses sprout the soil
The earth turns under the snow geese
Say hello to the elephant on the tip of
your nose

Host and guest together
Wiping off the mud.

Mind's Simple Emptiness

Eyes cannot see
 close and far together
Ears cannot hear
 both soft and loud
Nose cannot smell
 sweet and pungent at once
Tongue cannot taste
 sweet and sour the same
Touch cannot feel
 hot and cold as one.

But mind can do all,
 all this and
 all things
 from the beginingless beginning
 to the endless end
with mindlessness.

Simple emptiness.

Useless Words

Words are used to point
But words cannot express.
Words are the sickness of the mind
Healed only by what cannot be expressed.
Throw the dictionary in the furnace
And smell the water.

All There Is Is

Green leaves turn red.
Winter snows melt in spring.
Night and day are like one foot before the other.
The winds of the Absolute push the clouds.
All there is is this.
What else can there be?

Cannot Express

Let go of the glued pole
Let go of attachments
Gain nothing-to-gain
Grab hold of the passing cloud
Do not express what is

Clearness Soup

Build a pot of wisdom
Fill it with emptiness
Add a healthy dose of impermanence
Throw in lots of non-attachment.
Stir well in all directions
Pour into a glass of no-self.
Digest well.
Now...

Sleep when tired.
Eat when hungry.

Does Exist, Cannot Be Expressed

There are no separate objects before my
eyes;
The hole in the sky has been filled.
The gateless gate is on the head of a pin;
The stickiness of clinging is not.
The ground tells where to rake.
The ox stands still.

Nothing To Express

The hot winds of expressing
Blow the arrow off target.

No expressing.
No arrow.
No target.

Simply be.

The Freedom of Freedom

Empty the vast seas with a bottomless
bucket,
Wear down the mountains with the light
of the moon,
Swim upstream to the source of the
river of emptiness,
Throw away the mirror for the sake of
the wall,
Cool the furnace of desires.

Invite the sound of the bell
With its brother the gong
To offer
The freedom of freedom.

Dispelling the Cold Winter Inside

The frost on the many grasses
is slowly melted by the sun
rising from India
to warm the faces
from the long internal winter.

<u>Joining In</u>

Alone in this world
Returning to continue opening the lotus flower
Watching the clouds caress the mountains
Where the streams flow toward the great
ocean...

I join in.

Only Follow

On the sun's chariot, the seasons ride
The moon pulls, the seas swell
When bees arrive, plants grow.
All is unrehearsed.
All is universal.
Man is unable to compete.

Only follow.
Only practice.

Simple Treasure

All that is just is
Reality has no name
Grass is always green
The mountain snows melt in spring
Observe without attachment

Step to the Edge

Step to the near edge
To see the whole world below.
Let the spring winds blow
The lotus flower open
With what cannot be expressed.

A Raindrop Starts It All

A single rain drop
Begins a journey
With others to form
A stream,
A river,
An ocean.

A glint of understanding
Begins a journey
With others to form
A stream,
A river,
A shoreless ocean.

<u>Don't Know</u>

The mountains stroll by
The stream swims to the ocean
Vast is the "don't know".

Don't Seek Glory

Gold shines by itself.
Verification from others
Should never be sought.

False Clouds

Though trying to float
Many clouds are transparent
Seen through by the sun's
Truth of the ancients gone by.
Such clouds fool no one here.

False Practice

Cleaning mud with mud,
Kerosene with kerosene
Is the way of fools.
Follow the path of wisdom
With the untainted senses.

Natural Playing

The mist is playing
Tickling the mountain's whiskers.
Both giggle child-like,
Both play without playing.
Ah, there is no both anymore.

<u>No Thinking</u>

Go forward alone.
Stop being caught in thinking.
There is no-thing here.

<u>Nothing Is</u>

A fool can drown in an inch of water
But can be saved by the wisdom in the
depth of the sea.
The difference between the two is
awareness
That nothing is
As it seems.

Nothing Needed

Needing to attach
The tongue moves but adds nothing.
The sun warms us all.
Fishing with a hookless line,
Constant hunger is no more.

Nothing to Compare

No things are equal or separate
From end to end
Before the beginning and after the end
There is nothing to compare.
Walk through it eyes straight ahead.
Do not waiver.

Raining Cloud

The cloud slowly stops.
Peering through the haze of all
Blinking and hearing
While raining into the stream
Becoming one with the sea.

<u>Realization</u>

When the sun is born
The eyes open to see the real.
The wind moves the tree
Which stands its ground to live on
And shake with playful laughter.

<u>That's It!</u>

One flake of snow
Is touched by the red fireplace.
That's it!

The Journey

Life…
        is the journey.

The journey…
                is life.

Thieving Sensations

The moon reflected is not the truth,
A cloud does not go around twice.
False beliefs abound as snow covers the land.
Do not believe your sensations;
They are thieves in the dark of night
Leaving behind an empty house
Where there is no place to rest.

Your Path

Forget the path you seek.
Every breath and every step
Is your path.
Speaking about it hurts the ears.
The foot behind waits to move forward.
Don't block it with your mouth.

<u>This Is the Result</u>

This is the result of all events
      that has ever happened.
This is the result of all events
      that has not happened.
This is the result of all things
      that have never happened.
This is the result of all things
      that have not been.
This is the result of all causes
      that have ever caused.
This is the result of all causes
      that have never caused.
This is the result of all results
      that have ever been resulted.
This is the result of all results
      that have never resulted.

This is the Result.

I am the Result.

No Way

There is no pointing.
There is no pointing to anything
Other than pointing.

For being inexpressible
The pointed
Cannot be pointed at.

No Pleasure

What is pleasure?
Having no-pleasure to bare.
Alone come this way.

<u>Only A Dream</u>

It is but a dream
One where the dreamer fills all
So as not to awaken

<u>What You Are Not</u>

Only by understanding
What you are not,
Can you understand
What you are.

Endless Process of Being

Broken and shattered leaves
Brown and brittle with age
Swirl on the greyed pavement
Pushed about by the wind of life
In an endless process of being.

No "I"

One letter away from the truth
Numerous others on either side
Wide-eyed
Able to hear
In awe.

Working toward the letter
From both ends
Showing the falseness of even it.

There is no "I".

<u>Not Knowing</u>

Ignorance is here
Black clouds between sun and earth
Driving behavior
To the dark abyss of fear
Which soon boils into full greed.

The greed of humans
Is never seen by the rich
Or leaders
Ready to steal from the poor
Causing anger to boil on.

Anger turns violent
With nowhere to go but out
Inflicted on those
Who are ready to fight back
Closing the circle of fools.

All Being

Looking at the gong
Realizing I am the sound
Of it's friendship with the mallet.

False Notion

Self becomes selfish
Selfish becomes selfishness
Devious, impish
All based on a false notion
That all things are separate.

<u>Which Way?</u>

Your journey?
Never to start, never to end.
So...
Start it here
And...
Continue it here
And ride your white ox
Through the invisible gate
To see the wonders of the inside.

<u>All the Same</u>

The adobe houses speak to the light
passing wind.
"Where are you going?"
"Nowhere but here with you.
Coming. Going. All the same."

Endless Battle

The River of Fools
Continues to overflow
Well into the reefs
Of Greed, Anger, Ignorance
Where Darkness and Wind battle.

<u>No Need</u>

There is always a need for...
What?
Nothing.

Non-Transcending

How can there be a transcending of anything?
There is nothing to transcend!
No dust.
No mirror.
No reflection.

Only One Way

No cause or effect;
No plan to now go away;
Just a flowing stream;
Unified stream of events;
One continuous mistake.

<u>Simply Clear</u>

Clear understanding,
Known as an "enlightenment",
Is none other than...
The Oneness of the Absolute.
The knowing of One Moment.

Appearances

Appearances worn,
Taking the street called Nowhere.
Worn appearances.

Mind Thoughts

A wisp of dark smoke
Taken by the lightest wind;
The mind and its thoughts.

One Law

So please understand;
The Law of Impermanence
Decides all that is.

The Life of Kajin

My way is to abandon the self
By taking the path of the Self.
Rafting the Ocean of Impermanence
In the Land of the Absolute.
Letting nothing stick to my fingers
All for the sake of true freedom.
Travelling to the mountain top
And returning to the Original Valley.

Only This

As Moon waves goodbye,
Silence filters through the room
Filling this skin bag.
Sitting here on my cushion
There is no me...only this.

THIS
IS
NOT

THE
END.

IT
IS
ONLY

THE
BEGINNING

Pleasure Is......

(Began seeing in Mazangé, France April 1951...Began
writing on approach to Base Camp, Mera Peak, Nepal,
April 1998)
(Begun by Dan Landault...Continued as Kajin.)

Seeing stars shine knowing they are our
ancestors' candles lighting our path.

Watching the earth show us its beauty with the
opening of a flower.

Understanding that a shooting star or a comet's
tail is nature's fireworks.

The feeling of someone's glowing smile when
they have been helped by a stranger.

The beauty of a snow-covered mountain bathed
in shimmering moonlight.

A shadow chasing a running child on a sunny
afternoon.

A child, lollipop in hand, chasing birds.

Smelling the breeze after it has turned a hay
field into a flowing ocean of gold.

Having the eye of the Buddha twinkle your way
when life is hard.

Watching the Northern Lights dance with only the music of no-thinking to accompany them.

Companionship during your travels throughout life.

Knowing that a friend is concerned enough about you to call and give you hell and support at the same time.

Opening a bag of your favourite chips and lightly placing the first one on your tongue for your taste buds to enjoy.

Having good wine make love to your mouth knowing the work to make it and the history of this nectar.

Knowing that if your life ended tomorrow, no one should be sad, for you made someone smile.

Watching a river flow around obstacles and knowing it always gets to its destination in the end, intact.

The purr of a cat feeling warm and comfortable on your lap on a cool winter evening.

Watching an animal doing anything knowing that whatever it does is natural.

Watching the sun rise and the sun set knowing that they are both an end and a beginning to something.

Feeling the warmth of the sun on your cold skin even though both are only sensations.

Finally knowing that there is no such thing as reality.

Knowing the true meaning of Cause & Effect, the meaning of One, and truly experiencing Karma.

Seeing the help and support people offer others during trying and difficult times.

Learning valuable life-growing lessons from difficult experiences filled with pain.

Skiing down a powered slope with a focused, being-the-moment feeling of weightlessness.

Curling up under a warm blanket with a good book on a cold rainy day.

Holding your companion's hand, looking in her eyes and seeing the full beauty of the universe.

Sitting amongst a herd of Big Horn Sheep overlooking a mountain glacier on a warm sunny day.

Climbing.

The knowledge that the universe is unfolding as

it only can, in a natural state.

Watching companions go through life together while teaching and supporting each other, knowing you are one of them.

Watching your children grow into adults as they gain wisdom and knowing some of it came from you.

The comfort and protection of a tent after a hard day of climbing at altitude.

Accepting the fact that you are fallible, that you make mistakes and that you don't always have to be perfect.

Watching a cat nap, awaken, stretch, get up, turn around, lie back down and continue the nap.

Knowing that grass is green, a river flows, wind blows, the sun is bright and that these are as they should be, natural.

Being in the Himalayas among the people, scenery and mountains of Buddhist serenity.

Warm, dry clothes after a long, hard, wet day of trekking on a drizzly day in cold snow.

The simple things.

Getting over a cold.

Meditation.

Cycling a narrow twisted road with only the dust of past lives under your wheels.

Watching crows play in flight.

Simple friends.

The magic of life.

A field of sunflowers together, slowly, quietly following the sun's path.

Life.

Humour.

Hearing a meditation gong at 5 am in full, endless, and silent darkness.

Mindfulness.

Birds singing.

The scent of flowers.

Watching the bright red sun rise at Plum Village in France.

The rolling vineyard countryside of central France.

Watching a cat be a cat.

Silently riding bike.

Hearing the ancient echo of hoofs on stone streets in a medieval village in France.

Knowing what you are.

Knowing what you aren't.

Laughter.

Knowing that the answer to everything is…"Don't know."

Knowing that man will never control nature.

Making love.

Cycling the back roads of France on a quiet bike and hearing only heavy breathing.

Watching the miracle of loving closeness in two large white workhorses always needing to touch each other.

Watching a tired old man push his wife in a wheelchair on small roads for her to enjoy.

Living a dream with your companion.

Knowing that you are loved.

The wonderful smells of the coming meal.

Seeing the beauty of grey clouds.

Willow Tree dancing gently with it's friend, Wind.

Hearing from a friend about her travels.

Seeing a frown become a smile.

Watching the wind moving through but nothing to see.

A long belly-laugh.

A donkey eating carrots from your hand.

A lesson learned.

Knowing that water can be contained but not controlled.

Reflecting what is without judgment or alteration.

Watching five year old kids get excited about homemade bread made outside in a market in France.

Seeing good friends after a long absence.

Spring.

Rainbows.

Watching clouds travel.

The sensation of a gust of wind on your naked eyes.

Watching lightening chase the darkness away.

Wondering where the sound of the bell came from...and where it has gone.

Music reaching for the secrets of your heart.

Reconnecting with old friends, all of us roots of the same tree.

Riding the desert on a camel's river.

Playing with a little dog thrilled to be shown love.

The colours of the fall leaves.

Smelly, well-ripened French camembert cheese.

A crisp breeze caressing my red cheeks.

Feeding old bread to new birds.

Being adopted and loved by a sweet black cat in Los Escullos, Spain.

Knowing that total freedom is realizing that there is nothing to satisfy.

Understanding that the meaning of life is simply to live.

Being tightly and lovingly embraced by a beautiful friend.

The soft embracing sound of a monastery bell handed to me by the wind.

Sounding the pillow bell in the silent darkness.

The sands of the Sahara blowing across itself.

Feeling the disinterest of a camel in Morocco.

Sitting on the rim of Crater Lake.

The mass ascension of 500 balloons in Albuquerque, NM.

The simple beauty of nature in southern Utah.

Being held by Buddha in Sarnath.

The deep understanding of the Absolute.

Knowing, happily, that this is all there is...and it is only here.

Buddhism.

Zen.

Simplicity.

Before thoughts

The mind source

The Unborn

Silence

CPSIA information can be obtained
at www.ICGtesting.com
Printed in the USA
LVHW090540190719
624447LV00004B/3/P